FAMOUS FIGURES OF

BILLY THE KID

THE AMERICAN FRONTIER

FAMOUS FIGURES OF
THE AMERICAN FRONTIER

BILLY THE KID

BUFFALO BILL CODY

CRAZY HORSE

DAVY CROCKETT

GEORGE CUSTER

WYATT EARP

GERONIMO

JESSE JAMES

ANNIE OAKLEY

SITTING BULL

FAMOUS FIGURES OF

BILLY THE KID

THE AMERICAN FRONTIER

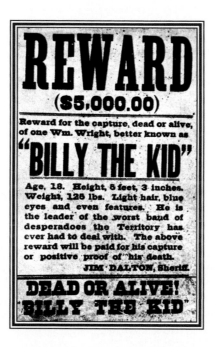

REWARD

($5,000.00)

Reward for the capture, dead or alive,
of one Wm. Wright, better known as

"BILLY THE KID"

Age, 18. Height, 5 feet, 3 inches.
Weight, 125 lbs. Light hair, blue
eyes and even features. He is
the leader of the worst band of
desperadoes the Territory has
ever had to deal with. The above
reward will be paid for his capture
or positive proof of his death.

JIM DALTON, Sheriff.

DEAD OR ALIVE!
BILLY THE KID

Daniel E. Harmon

Chelsea House Publishers
Philadelphia

Produced for Chelsea House by
OTTN Publishing, Stockton, NJ

CHELSEA HOUSE PUBLISHERS
Editor in Chief: Sally Cheney
Associate Editor in Chief: Kim Shinners
Production Manager: Pamela Loos
Art Director: Sara Davis
Series Designer: Keith Trego

First Printing

1 3 5 7 9 8 6 4 2

The Chelsea House World Wide Web address is
http://www.chelseahouse.com

Library of Congress Cataloging-in-Publication Data

Harmon, Daniel E.
Billy the Kid / by Daniel E. Harmon.
    p.   cm. – (Famous figures of the American frontier)
Includes bibliographical references and index.
Summary: Examines the life and exploits of Billy the Kid, an
infamous bandit of the Old West.
    ISBN 0-7910-6483-2 (alk. paper)
    ISBN 0-7910-6484-0 (pbk.: alk. paper)
1. Billy the Kid–Juvenile literature. 2. Outlaws–Southwest,
New–Biography–Juvenile literature. 3. Frontier and pioneer
life–Southwest, New–Juvenile literature. 4. Southwest, New–
Biography–Juvenile literature. [1. Billy the Kid. 2. Robbers
and Outlaws.] I. Title. II. Series.

F786.B54 H37 2001
364.15'52'09–dc21
[B]   2001028864

CONTENTS

A mural painting of Billy the Kid, the West's most infamous outlaw. Although hundreds of stories have been told about the Kid, the events of his life and death are surrounded in mystery and legend.

THE MYSTERY KID

In November 1950, news reporters in Texas filed an astonishing story. An aging, graying man named William Henry Roberts in the small town of Hamilton wanted to talk to the governor of neighboring New Mexico. Roberts had applied for a *pardon*–official forgiveness for violent crimes he said he had committed as a young man.

What crimes? the governor and the public were curious to know. Roberts was not on any law enforcement agency's wanted list.

The crimes of Billy the Kid! Roberts claimed to be the infamous outlaw.

It seemed almost impossible. History books said Billy the Kid had been shot to death by Sheriff Pat Garrett almost 70 years before. In 1950, if still alive, Billy would have been around 90 years old.

Other men during the early 20th century had claimed to be Billy the Kid. Some wanted to bask in misbegotten fame–perhaps to make money giving lectures and publishing books. Others simply wanted to see if they could pull off elaborate jokes on the press and public. Obviously, not all of them could be the real Billy the Kid. Historians marked them all down as *impostors* or pranksters.

Yet, a number of features about Roberts seemed to suggest he could have been the "boy bandit" made famous in books and songs, movies and plays. For example, he knew a lot about the lawless years when Billy the Kid roamed the badlands of eastern New Mexico. He was particularly familiar with certain buildings and places around Lincoln, New Mexico, that would have been familiar to the Kid.

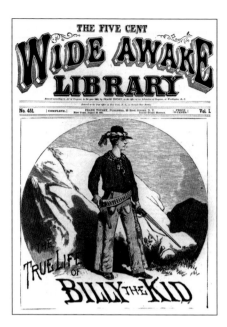

The story of Billy the Kid has fascinated people of all ages for more than 120 years. This magazine edition of the life of Billy the Kid was published in August 1881, a month after the outlaw was shot to death by Pat Garrett.

Many of the things Roberts described, some researchers believe, could have been known only by someone who had been involved at the time.

Roberts was similar in size to the Kid, based on what people knew of Billy's height and build. Of special interest were Roberts's hands and wrists. One of Billy's legendary feats was his ability to wiggle free of handcuffs because of his small hands. Roberts could tuck his thumbs in such an odd way that his hands became smaller around than his wrists. This would make handcuffs useless on him.

There was even more convincing evidence: Roberts had scars on his body, possibly from old bullet and knife wounds. These matched the body locations where historians thought Billy had been wounded in fights. Then there were ***testimonials***, signed statements by respectable elderly people who vowed they had known Billy the Kid during and after his wild young years. They swore William Henry Roberts was the Kid. One man who claimed he had ridden with the bandit said he could tell Roberts and Billy were the same because of their odd-colored eyes. A woman said her husband once sold horses to Billy the Kid; when she saw the aging Roberts, she recognized him from the old days.

Roberts seemed to be an honest man. According to William V. Morrison, a legal researcher who brought Roberts to public attention, all his life the old man had denied being Billy the Kid. Whenever he met people who recognized him as the Kid, he would tell them they were mistaken. When Morrison himself first interviewed him, Roberts claimed he was not the Kid. But then, realizing Morrison might be able to help win his pardon, Roberts told his story.

Most western researchers still doubt Brushy Bill Roberts's story. They believe Roberts was one of many pretenders who claimed to have been Billy the Kid.

The New Mexico governor questioned

William Henry Roberts in November 1950. Afterward, the governor refused to grant a pardon, because he didn't believe Roberts actually was Billy the Kid. A month later, Roberts died of heart failure.

Whichever story you believe, the claim of William Henry Roberts points out one certain fact: Billy the Kid–like many colorful characters on the American *frontier*–is a man of mystery. When you examine his story, it's difficult to tell fact from fable.

In many cases, America's trailblazers, frontier builders, lawmen, and bad men couldn't record their own deeds because they were **illiterate**. Others simply were not interested in keeping diaries. If they were interviewed by journalists, they tended to invent outlandish tales of daring. The journalists did their own share of exaggerating, hoping to sell more newspapers and books. Eyewitnesses were unreliable, sometimes giving conflicting information to different interviewers. Meanwhile, public records of frontier events were not very thorough.

So there is no way to know exactly what happened–or how, or why–in the New Mexico territory during the 1870s and early 1880s. What follows is the basic story, as we know it, of the life and death of Billy the Kid.

This is one of the few actual photographs taken of Billy the Kid. According to descriptions of the outlaw, Billy was short, standing just five feet seven inches high. He had a young-looking face and was always smiling, acquaintances said. A rancher friend named Frank Coe described the Kid as "a free-hearted, generous boy. He'd give a friend the shirt off his back."

A FRIENDLY YOUNG MAN

He was a likeable lad. People weren't afraid of him because he was small and he liked to laugh. They felt sorry for him because he was an orphan. But behind the boyish grin, William H. Bonney was a bundle of trouble. During a four-year period, from 1877 to 1881, he made a name for himself that would live forever in the history of violent crime: Billy the Kid.

Not much is known about his childhood. Historians believe he was born in New York in 1859 or 1860 and that his parents were from Ireland. His mother's name was Katherine McCarty Bonney; his father was William Bonney. Most researchers agree that the youth's given name was Henry (the "H." in William H. Bonney undoubtedly stood for "Henry"). But by the time he was in his mid-teens, he was calling himself "Billy"–his stepfather's name. He sometimes identified himself as Billy McCarty, sometimes as Billy Antrim.

Some say he was an ***illegitimate*** child (meaning his parents were not married) who never knew his father. Others say his father died when Henry was very young. Biographers record that he may have had an older brother named Joseph or a younger brother, Edward. When the boys were small, their mother reportedly moved west with her children to Indiana, then to Kansas. She owned a laundry in Wichita, Kansas, and stayed busy while her sons played in the dusty streets.

In 1873, his mother married a man named William Antrim, and the family eventually moved to Silver City, New Mexico. Antrim was a bartender and ***prospector*** who was almost never home.

When Billy was 14, his mother died of tuberculosis, a lung disease known in those days as "consumption." She had been sick for years, and her condition probably was the reason she had moved to the Southwest. She hoped the warm, dry air would help her improve. Mrs. Antrim's disease was too far advanced, though. She spent the last four months of her life confined to bed, growing weaker each day.

When Billy's mother Katherine married William Antrim, the family moved to this house in Silver City, New Mexico.

Sheriff Pat Garrett, Billy's onetime friend who eventually became his deadly enemy, wrote a book about the Kid after Billy's death. In it, Garrett reported that the young boy showed "a spirit of reckless daring, yet generous and tender feeling." But "his temper was fearful, and in his angry moods he was dangerous."

Garrett recounted that Billy first killed a man when he was only 12 years old. Rushing to the aid of a friend in a barroom fight, Billy stabbed a man with a knife, Garrett reported. Most modern-day western historians doubt this ever occurred, but the incident was widely repeated in newspapers and books after Billy's death.

Garrett recorded many other exciting, often violent adventures about Billy as a teenager: fights with Indians and Mexicans, high-speed chases on horseback, the rescue of a wagon train from an Apache attack. Garrett supposedly heard these sto-

One of Billy's favorite weapons was this Colt .44 revolver—a gun that was commonly used by lawmen in the West as well.

ries directly from the Kid. Again, many historians doubt they really happened.

After they were orphaned, Billy and his brother were taken in by Silver City citizens and began performing odd jobs. Billy wasn't

> Billy was a brave young man with iron nerves. He was a good shot with a pistol and rifle, a fast thinker, agile and active. One of his friends, a rancher named Frank Coe, later recalled, "Billy was a great hunter.... [He] could hit a bear's eye so far away I could hardly see the bear."

known as a bad boy. In fact, one of his employers claimed Billy was the only honest youngster who ever worked for him. Billy's schoolteacher reportedly liked him because he offered to do chores for her.

Some historians believe Billy was barely able to read and write. Others say he was an avid reader who also loved music and dancing. His favorite tune was said to be "Turkey in the Straw." His friend Frank Coe reported after Billy's death that the Kid could read and write and spoke with good grammar.

Billy got into childish trouble like other boys. He never came to the attention of the police, though, until he was 15.

The incident that first landed him in jail was not

really his doing. A man in town stole some clothes from a Chinese laundryman as a practical joke and persuaded Billy to hide them. Billy was caught and locked in jail. It was a horrible experience for the boy, but it taught him one way to take care of himself. Because of his small size, he was able to crawl up the chimney and get away. It was the first of several successful escapes for Billy, who from that moment on lived his life as a *fugitive*—an outlaw.

After his breakout, Billy ran away. He got jobs tending cattle and sheep, and made his way westward to Arizona. There he got a job as a **teamster** at an army lumber camp. His job was to drive the mules that hauled the logs from forest to sawmill.

For a while, he led a fairly normal frontier life. He was becoming known as a petty thief, however. He even stole horses, a serious crime in the West.

Then, in August 1877, his behavior turned violent. He got into a fight with a brawny man named Frank "Windy" Cahill, the camp's blacksmith. Cahill called Billy a bad name, Billy returned the insult, and Cahill knocked him down. Billy drew his pistol and fired—an act of self-defense, according to witnesses. Cahill died the next day. He probably was the first man killed by Billy the Kid.

By the late 1870s, cattle ranching had become a profitable business in the Southwest. Ranchers could expect to make 9 or 10 times their initial investment. Easterners and European investors—many from the British Isles, such as John Tunstall—were inspired to buy ranches in the American West and begin raising cattle.

Although he may have been defending himself, Billy was locked in the camp guardhouse. Again, he managed to escape after several days. But now, at 17, he was on the run not for taking part in a prank theft but for a shooting death. He returned to New Mexico and started calling himself William Bonney (which some researchers believe was his real name). By now, though, he was better known by an *alias* that would never be forgotten: Billy the Kid.

Billy was about the age of a high school senior when he went to work for a rancher named John Tunstall near Lincoln, in southeastern New Mexico. Lincoln was a hard frontier town of mostly Mexican-style *adobe* houses. There were bandits, gamblers, and drunks who often fought and killed one another. Unmarked graves could be seen in some of the yards and orchards; few people remembered the names of the gunfight victims who occupied them.

Young Bonney naturally did the same things as the others around him. Biographers doubt he was a heavy drinker, but he loved to gamble and squandered much of the money he made *cowpunching* or stealing. His favorite card game was *monte*. The beardless young man became so good at monte that from time to time saloonkeepers hired him as a card dealer.

Few people lived in the vast county. Those who did were from various backgrounds. There were many

Western historian Robert M. Utley, the author of a biography of Billy the Kid, wrote that the Lincoln County folk "labored at an honest living but stood ready to break the law when opportunity presented."

Hispanics; Caucasians came from the East and from California; African-American soldiers made up much of the **garrison** at Fort Stanton, nine miles from Lincoln on the Rio Bonito; and Mescalero Apaches lived on a nearby reservation. The various classes did not always get along well together. When men stumbled through the batwing saloon doors, dazed with whiskey, fights were bound to occur.

In most cases, no one was arrested when violence broke out. If those who committed crimes were arrested, they easily could escape the laughable Lincoln jail. If they didn't escape, they were almost certain to be found innocent by a jury of their **peers**—mostly lawless men like themselves. Even citizens who were basically honest figured the rugged frontier had its own set of rules to live by.

Tunstall, Billy's boss in Lincoln, was a "foreigner" from England. Some of the people in Lincoln County liked him—but Tunstall also made powerful enemies. When the tension came to a head in what was called the Lincoln County War, Billy the Kid found himself right in the middle of it.

Lawrence G. Murphy (right) and James J. "Jimmy" Dolan (left) were two of the most powerful men in Lincoln County, New Mexico. When a rancher named John Tunstall attempted to break their control of the county, Murphy and Dolan had him murdered.

THE LINCOLN COUNTY WAR

The Lincoln County War was a feud between two groups of cattle ranchers and businessmen on the southwestern frontier. The fighters were not soldiers but *gunslingers*. They were not fighting for freedom or rights or boundaries or defense. They were fighting for wealth, power, and revenge.

According to most accounts, Lawrence G. Murphy

was a retired army officer from California who settled in the Pecos River territory of New Mexico. He,
along with some partners, owned a Lincoln saloon
and a large general store called "The House" or the
"Big Store." It was probably the grandest, most
thriving general merchandise business in the eastern
part of New Mexico territory. Murphy also owned a
ranch outside Lincoln.

Murphy and his business partner, J. J. "Jimmy"
Dolan, became wealthy, largely by selling beef to
the U.S. Army. They made many friends, including
the Lincoln County sheriff, William Brady. This was
a very good thing for Murphy, because everyone
knew the cowhands Murphy hired for his ranch
were stealing cattle from surrounding herds.
Whenever the Murphy/Dolan men were accused of
stealing, the sheriff did not seem very interested in
arresting them. If these *rustlers* ever were arrested,
they were always found innocent by local juries—
which mostly consisted of men who did some
rustling themselves.

John Chisum was the most powerful rancher in
the region. He reportedly owned as many as 80,000
cows and grazed them along the Pecos for a distance
of 150 miles. His herd was so big he could not

John Tunstall was a wealthy 24-year-old from England. Like John Chisum, a fellow rancher, Tunstall felt that Murphy and Dolan had no right to interfere with his business. When he set up a store in Lincoln to compete with the shop operated by Murphy and Dolan, the men ordered his execution.

protect it very effectively. Dishonest ranchers often stole Chisum's *stock*, claiming the animals were strays. Murphy's rustlers were especially troublesome to Chisum.

Another rancher in Lincoln County was Billy the Kid's boss, John Tunstall. A friend of John Chisum, the Englishman had come west to find adventure. Tunstall opened a general store of his own in Lincoln. Soon, his store was attracting many of Murphy's customers.

As you might expect, this infuriated Murphy. The tension between the two men increased when Murphy lost a court case in which he expected to inherit some valuable property. The opposing lawyer, Alexander McSween, was a friend of Tunstall. He may have been Tunstall's partner in running the general store.

Enraged, Murphy had his friend Sheriff Brady send a *posse* to Tunstall's ranch. They had orders to take some of Tunstall's cattle to repay Murphy for his lost inheritance. They were also ordered to bring Tunstall into town.

Surprisingly, Tunstall apparently agreed to go with them. On the road between Tunstall's ranch and Lincoln, the men in the posse shot and killed Tunstall. The slaying, committed in February 1878, was witnessed by some of Tunstall's cowhands. One of them, according to most accounts, was Billy the Kid. Billy and his companions knew the legal authorities in Lincoln were unlikely to enforce justice, so

The murder of John Tunstall was probably committed in cold blood, although the members of the posse later claimed Tunstall had drawn his pistol and shot at them first.

they plotted revenge for the death of their boss and personal friend.

Tunstall's foreman Dick Brewer, Billy, and an unknown number of other cowboys (as many as 60, at the height of the war) set about to enforce justice themselves. They were acting as **vigilantes**, citizens who appoint themselves to enforce the law. Billy and his friends called themselves the Regulators.

To some extent, they had legal backing for their mission of vengeance. A ***justice of the peace*** in Lincoln was alarmed by Tunstall's murder and was pressured by the public outcry for justice. He deputized Brewer, Billy, and others for the specific purpose of finding Tunstall's killers.

Their activities as deputies hardly cast them as heroes, though. In fact, there were no heroes in the Lincoln County War. Billy and his companions were known to be rustlers and rowdies in their own right. They behaved little better than the members of the posse that murdered John Tunstall.

Prowling the canyons and riverbanks of the New Mexico frontier, they set up **ambushes** and shot their enemies without warning. After capturing two of Tunstall's murderers and promising them safe conduct to Lincoln for trials, they shot the men on the trail–claiming later the prisoners had tried to escape. If they suspected a man of being a member of the posse that had shot Tunstall, that man was in danger of losing his life–as were those around him.

In one encounter, Billy and his friends

ambushed and killed Sheriff Brady in the streets of Lincoln. Billy, too, received a bullet wound that day; one of Brady's companions shot him in the thigh. Billy recovered, but the cold-blooded killing of Brady turned many of Billy's friends against him. Sheriff Brady's death, in the public mind, made an outlaw of the young man who until then had been just another cowhand and sometime rustler and gunslinger in the rowdy, untamed Southwest.

Billy still had friends in Lincoln—people who did not like the way the Murphy and Dolan crowd operated. He hid with some of these friends for several weeks until he was well enough to ride again. During that time, the sheriff's deputies were looking for him everywhere. In one close call, witnesses later reported, he hid inside a wooden barrel in a Mexican woman's kitchen. She prepared a meal on top of it as lawmen searched her house.

In July 1878, Murphy's men surrounded the Lincoln home of McSween, the lawyer, while Billy and other members of his gang were inside. For several days, the two sides taunted and shot at each other. Finally, the Murphy men set the house aflame. McSween was shot when he emerged from the smoke-filled doorway. Billy, however, managed to escape, shooting at least one of Murphy's men.

Billy continued his campaign of revenge. In time, he and his friends killed many of the members of Murphy's posse. Murphy himself began losing money—he found that his hired gunmen were costing him more than he could make rustling. He died a broken man. His partner Jimmy Dolan went bankrupt.

According to some chronicles of the Lincoln County War, the deadly assault on the McSween home was witnessed by a U.S. Army troop. The soldiers allegedly stood by and did nothing to prevent the attack. Some sources claim the soldiers even joined in the shooting against McSween and his friends.

With the deaths of Tunstall, McSween, and Murphy, the Lincoln County War ended. The survivors of the two factions either verbally agreed to stop fighting or simply avoided further conflicts with each other.

It's difficult to say which side won—or whether either side won. The Kid had gotten a measure of revenge for Tunstall's murder, but he had lost any chance to lead a settled life. He would be an outlaw for as long as he lived. And his time was growing very, very short.

Lew Wallace had been a general in the Union army during the Civil War. In 1878 he was appointed territorial governor of New Mexico. Hoping to end the violence of the Lincoln County War, he offered Billy the Kid a pardon if he would surrender and testify against other participants in the fighting.

ON THE RUN

Before the Lincoln County War, some researchers believe, Billy and a close friend named Fred Waite had talked of eventually becoming law-abiding farmers on the Rio Peñasco. But after the fighting was over, Billy—now wanted for several murders—took to cattle rustling for a living. Events—and his own poor judgment—had conspired to force the Kid to continue his life of crime.

Billy the Kid kills a shop-keeper ally of Dolan and Murphy during the Lincoln County War in this 19th-century *Police Gazette* sketch. Though Billy once claimed to have killed 21 men—one for every year of his life—most historians believe the actual number of men he murdered was seven.

His behavior, though, wasn't determined completely by outside forces beyond his control. If he ever wanted something, an acquaintance recalled, he would simply take it, no questions asked.

In 1879, Billy briefly thought he might be given a second chance. Lew Wallace, a former Civil War general, had been appointed by President Rutherford B. Hayes to be governor of the New Mexico Territory. Wallace found that some parts of the territory, such as Lincoln County, were so wild and lawless that circuit judges "dared not hold court." He wanted to put an end to the violence that made the area an awful place to live.

Wallace decided to punish the ring of business-men who had ordered the murder of John Tunstall and started the Lincoln County War. In order to bring the killers to justice, though, he needed an eyewitness, someone who had seen the crime and was brave enough to talk about it under oath. If Billy the Kid would turn himself in and testify in court against his old enemies, Wallace promised, the governor would throw out all the murder warrants against Billy. "I will let you go scot free with a pardon in your pocket for all your misdeeds," he promised Billy.

After thinking about the offer for a long time, Billy agreed. He let himself be arrested on a minor charge, with the understanding that he soon would be found innocent and set free with a full pardon.

While awaiting trial, he testified in court against the Lincoln County conspirators. Two of them were charged with murder.

However, the district attorney, William Rynerson, refused to let

During the time of Billy the Kid's pardon agreement with Lew Wallace, and his later arrest and escape, the governor was writing the final chapters of a novel. The book would later be published to much acclaim. Its title: *Ben Hur.*

Billy go. Rynerson had been a supporter of the Murphy faction during the Lincoln County War. The men Billy had helped convict were allowed to go free, but Rynerson sent Billy back to jail. Billy was to be tried for killing Sheriff Brady.

Naturally, Billy was furious. He had indeed murdered the crooked sheriff and deserved to be punished. But he had the governor's own promise of *amnesty* in exchange for his court *testimony*.

For several months, Billy wrote letter after letter to Governor Wallace, demanding his freedom. Wallace refused to order his release or even to answer his letters. The governor confided to a reporter, "I can't see how a fellow like him should expect any clemency [pardon] from me."

Governor Wallace offered a $500 reward to anyone who could catch Billy the Kid.

BILLY THE KID.

$500 REWARD.

I will pay $500 reward to any person or persons who will capture William Bonny, alias The Kid, and deliver him to any sheriff of New Mexico. Satisfactory proofs of identity will be required.

LEW. WALLACE,
Governor of New Mexico.

However, some citizens of Lincoln County felt the reward was too small. They criticized the governor and promised to give an extra $1,000 to Billy's captor. A new sheriff, Billy's former friend Pat Garrett, would soon ride in search of the elusive outlaw.

Finally, realizing the governor was not going to help him, Billy escaped, slipping his small wrists out of his handcuffs.

The governor's betrayal made Billy a very dangerous enemy. Susan Wallace, the governor's wife, stated in a letter that "we hold our lives at the mercy of desperadoes and outlaws, chief among them Billy the Kid." She reported that Billy had sworn to kill the lawmen and politicians—including Wallace—who had lied to him, then "surrender and be hanged."

Governor Wallace now decided something must be done—not to help Billy, but to guard against him. He offered a $500 reward for the Kid's recapture. To bring him in, an especially tough and wise lawman was set on Billy's trail.

PAT GARRETT

After escaping, Billy the Kid hid out near Fort Sumner, New Mexico, on the Pecos River. During this time he struck up a friendship with Pat Garrett, a bartender at a saloon in Fort Sumner. In 1880, Garrett was elected sheriff of Lincoln County; he was ordered to track down and capture Billy the Kid.

A Friend Turns Enemy

Compared with Billy the Kid, Patrick Floyd Garrett was a giant. He stood six feet four inches, nine inches taller than Billy. They were different in most other ways, too. Billy liked to joke, laugh, and brag about his deeds. Garrett was soft-spoken, and, although easy to get along with, he said little. Yet, the two had become friends while working as cowboys.

Pat Garrett was born in Alabama in 1850. At 19, he went to Texas and spent seven years as a cow-puncher, buffalo hunter, and Indian fighter. One of his friends from those years later reported that Garrett disliked fighting the Comanches. Garrett reasoned that the natives, after all, had first claim to the territory. However, the Comanches' raids threat-ened the security of families along the frontier and had to be stopped.

In 1878, Garrett left Texas and found work as a cowboy on a ranch near Fort Sumner, New Mexico, on the banks of the Pecos River—the stomping grounds of Billy the Kid. Garrett reportedly saved enough of his cowboy wages to buy a tiny restau-rant, then go into partnership with the owner of a Fort Sumner saloon. While Garrett worked there as a bartender, a cowboy named Charlie Bowdre intro-duced Garrett to Billy. The two men became friends.

Garrett married a Spanish-American woman named Apolinaria Gutierrez in January 1880. He became very popular along the Pecos among both the American ranchers and the Mexican-American citizens. In autumn 1880, some of the leading cattle-men like John Chisum talked him into running for sheriff of Lincoln County. Thanks to their influence,

Garrett was elected by a large margin.

One of the first things his backers wanted him to do was solve the problem of Billy the Kid's rustling. Soon after he was elected, Garrett reportedly paid Billy a visit. He hoped they still could be friends, Garrett said, but the thefts would have to stop.

The warning didn't persuade Billy to change his ways. It soon became clear that the new sheriff would have to arrest the Kid. Garrett was not eager to set out after Billy and his gang–most of whom Garrett had joked and played cards with in happier times. They were his friends.

Throughout autumn 1880, the new sheriff and a posse searched for Billy and his gang. Whenever Garrett would enter a town and ask whether anyone had seen the Kid, he usually was given false information. Many of the people admired Billy for his raids against the big cattle ranchers. Others were afraid to talk because they feared him. If they knew where the outlaw was, they would pretend they did not–or they would send the posse off in the wrong direction.

Garrett understood what was going on. He set traps for Billy by spreading false information about where his posse would look next. The lawmen came

A sheriff's posse tracks outlaws in this 19th-century illustration. Although Pat Garrett did not want to arrest his friend, he set many traps for Billy the Kid while following the wanted man from 1880–81.

close several times, and in December they surprised the gang at Fort Sumner in a night snowstorm. One of Billy's best friends, Tom O'Folliard, was killed. But the Kid and the rest of the gang escaped.

The sheriff guessed where they would go: a deserted adobe cabin at a remote place called Stinking Springs. Located outside of town, it was the only place within many miles where the outlaws could find shelter from the snow and the bitter cold.

Garrett arrived at the cabin just before daylight on December 23, 1880, and divided his 12 men into two groups. They surrounded the little hut, which had no windows and an open, doorless entrance. Billy and his men had taken two of the horses into the dark cabin with them to help them stay warm. The other animals were tethered outside.

When one of the bandits came outside to feed the horses at dawn, the posse shot him. Garrett saw to his dismay that it was Charlie Bowdre, the old friend who had introduced him to Billy. Bowdre only days before had hinted at turning himself in and quitting the outlaw life.

The two sides settled down for a long, cheerless *siege*. Sometimes Garrett and the Kid chatted with each other across the way. But Garrett could not talk Billy into surrendering.

Late in the afternoon, the posse came up with an idea. They began roasting large slices of raw beef over their open fire and brewing pots of hot coffee. The men inside the adobe hut had no fire and almost no food at all. They were starving, and the warm aroma from the posse's feast settled the issue. One by one, Billy and his comrades emerged with their hands up. The lawmen took away their guns, then let them enjoy a supper of steak and hot coffee.

Billy the Kid was in custody at last.

ROBT. M. OLLINGER
DIED HERE
KILLED BY BILLY THE KID
APRIL 28. 1881

After his arrest by Pat Garrett, Billy was held on the second floor of the Lincoln County Courthouse, pictured on the opposite page. With little hope of receiving a pardon, on April 28, 1881, Billy slipped his hand-cuffs, killed guards Robert Olinger (whose name is some-times spelled with two "l"s) and J. W. Bell, and escaped.

One Last Moment of Freedom

In April 1881, the Kid was tried and convicted in Mesilla for the murder of Sheriff William Brady (although the fatal shot in the Brady ambush possibly had been fired by one of Billy's friends). Billy was transferred to Lincoln to be hanged.

One of the most mysterious and infamous jailbreaks in American history occurred on April 28, 1881. Billy

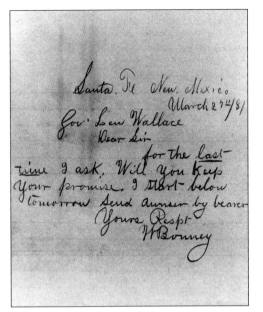

While waiting in jail, Billy wrote numerous letters to Lew Wallace, asking the governor to keep his end of their bargain and grant him a pardon. This letter, signed with his family name, W. H. Bonney, was written a month before Billy escaped.

the Kid was being held on the second floor of the Lincoln County Courthouse, awaiting his date with the hangman just two weeks away. Although he was shackled hand and foot, he somehow obtained a weapon, killed his two guards, filed off his irons, and rode out of town alone.

Deputy Sheriff J. W. Bell, one of the slain guards, was said to be a kind-hearted man who treated the prisoner fairly. Billy hated the other guard, though. He was Deputy Marshal Robert Olinger, an old enemy from the Lincoln County War.

Olinger had taken some other prisoners across the street for a meal at a Lincoln hotel. Bell was left alone to guard Billy. Some people believe one of

Billy's friends had left a pistol hidden for him in the outhouse, a small, crude, wooden bathroom building behind the jail. Others believe he managed to steal Bell's own gun. Whatever the case, Billy shot the deputy dead.

Sympathizers of the "boy bandit" doubt he wanted to shoot Deputy Bell, but when the deputy tried to stop him, it cost Bell his life. Critics, however, assume Billy shot the officer in cold blood.

Olinger came running back across the street after he heard the gunshots. Billy was waiting for him with Olinger's own double-barrel shotgun. He shot Olinger without giving him a chance to draw a weapon. The townspeople were so terrified by the sudden killings that they did nothing to try to keep Billy from getting away.

Sheriff Pat Garrett was in the town of White Oaks when he learned of the incredible escape. Naturally, he was bent on bringing the Kid back to justice and avenging his slain deputies. For the moment, though, all he could do was wait for someone to report Billy's whereabouts.

"I stayed at home, most of the time, and busied myself about the ranch," Garrett later wrote. Many citizens criticized him for apparently doing nothing–perhaps he was afraid of Billy, they said. But that was exactly what Sheriff Garrett wanted them to believe. If word reached the Kid that Garrett was not trying very hard to find him, Billy might become overconfident and come out of hiding.

Garrett at last heard from a reliable rancher that Billy was in Fort Sumner. Then the sheriff played a trick. He and two deputies, John W. Poe and Thomas K. McKinney, took a trip away from Fort Sumner toward the town of Roswell–but by night they secretly turned back. For three days and nights they kept to forgotten trails near the Pecos River. No one saw them when they arrived near Fort Sumner or even guessed they were in the area.

The lawmen believed a rancher named Pete "Pedro" Maxwell would give them honest information about Billy the Kid's movements. Maxwell had been Garrett's boss when Garrett first came to New Mexico as a cowhand. The rancher was widely respected.

Garrett and his deputies slipped close to the Maxwell ranch after midnight on July 14, 1881. The ranch house was dark; Maxwell was obviously asleep. Garrett quietly went inside and sat down at the side of the rancher's bed. He woke Maxwell and

Pat Garrett, wearing a hat, shoots Billy the Kid in the bedroom of Pete Maxwell, as Maxwell bolts from his bed. This illustration originally appeared in the first edition of Pat Garrett's 1882 book about his former friend, *An Authentic Life of Billy the Kid.*

asked if he knew where the ***desperado*** might be.

Amazingly, Billy the Kid himself was staying at the ranch. He had been living in a cowhand's cabin outside. Even more astoundingly, at that moment Billy was walking, bareheaded and sock-footed, into the main house with a butcher knife in his hand. He wanted to cut himself a late-night snack of beef in the kitchen.

Garrett's two deputies, waiting on the porch outside, had no idea the half-dressed man who walked past them and entered the house was Billy the Kid. They didn't know Billy was around. They figured the late-night visitor must be a Mexican ranch hand.

In the darkness, neither Garrett nor Billy realized who the other was. They sensed each other's presence, though. "That's him!" the frightened rancher hissed, rolling to safety on the floor beside his bed. The sheriff drew his pistol and fired. His bullet struck Billy the Kid in the breast.

"He never spoke," Garrett later wrote of the dying outlaw. "A struggle or two, a little strangling sound as he gasped for breath, and the Kid was with his many victims."

Billy may have died not knowing who shot him. Believing the sheriff was many miles away, he had been moving about freely at the Maxwell ranch and in Fort Sumner. He'd received no warning that the clever Garrett was back in the area. In the moment before Garrett fired the fatal bullet in Pete Maxwell's bedroom, Billy had been backing away, shouting, "*¿Quién es? ¿Quién es?*"–Spanish for "Who's that?" Billy, who spoke excellent Spanish, apparently thought the mysterious third person in the bedroom was a Mexican. Had the Kid known it was Garrett, he undoubtedly would

> Some historians believe Billy never had a chance to fire his pistol. If he did, no bullet or bullet hole was ever found in the bedroom.

have fired his pistol instantly.

For his part, Garrett didn't realize the person who entered the door was Billy until seconds before the shooting began. He at first thought it must be Maxwell's brother-in-law. Only when Maxwell breathed, "That's him!" did it dawn on Garrett that he had accidentally found the young outlaw he'd been chasing.

An inquest was held the next morning. The coroner's jury pronounced that the dead man was William H. Bonney and that he had died from a bullet fired by Sheriff Garrett in the line of duty—"justifiable homicide." The jury concluded that Garrett "deserves to be rewarded."

Interestingly, Governor Wallace again went back on his word, refusing to give Garrett the posted $500 reward money. Some of Billy's old enemies, though, raised several thousand dollars as a personal reward for the sheriff. Eventually, the territorial legislature passed an act granting Garrett the original reward.

Billy the Kid was buried in the army cemetery at Fort Sumner.

The afternoon sun falls over Billy the Kid's grave in Fort Sumner, New Mexico. He is buried with two of his friends, Charlie Bowdre and Tom O'Folliard.

How Much of the Legend Is True?

That is the story of Billy the Kid as it commonly is told . . . and retold.

Someone once made a very interesting comment about the Kid: he is more famous than most American presidents. It's true. Many Americans don't know that men like John Tyler, Benjamin Harrison, and William McKinley were U.S. presidents. But most Americans—

and many people in foreign countries–know Billy the Kid was an outlaw.

Yet, during the 120 years since his death, getting the true story of his short life has not been easy. More than 800 books have been written about Billy the Kid, and yet few fresh details about his life and deeds have come to light in more than a century.

Eight books about the outlaw were published in the months after his death. Some were instant best-sellers, but they were based largely on rumors and on the writers' active imaginations.

To correct these flawed and outright false accounts, Sheriff Garrett wrote his own biography of Billy the Kid the year after their deadly encounter. A journalist named Ashmun Upson helped him write it. Parts of the book seem overly dramatic and exaggerated, and some historians believe Garrett himself mainly wanted to make money from Billy the Kid's national popularity. Still, it remains one of the main sources of information we have today about the tragic young man.

The sheriff said that although Billy the Kid committed horrible crimes, he also had a kind streak and wanted desperately to be understood. While Billy was in jail, the two of them, according to Garrett, had several heart-to-heart conversations. Garrett said that Billy expressed no anger toward his onetime friend for arresting him.

To the end, Billy impressed people as being just "a boy." A newspaper reporter who interviewed him in jail about six months before his death wrote that he looked "like a school boy. . . . He is, in all, quite a handsome looking fellow, the only imperfection being two prominent front teeth slightly protruding like squirrel's teeth, and he has agreeable and winning ways."

> "Those who knew him best will tell you that in his most savage and dangerous moods his face always wore a smile," Pat Garrett wrote in his biography of Billy the Kid. "He ate and laughed, drank and laughed, rode and laughed, talked and laughed, fought and laughed–and killed and laughed."

Some historians place little value on Garrett's biography of the Kid. W. C. Jameson, for example, is a professor and author who believes Billy the Kid may have been William Henry Roberts, the elderly man who came to public attention almost 70 years after the Fort Sumner shoot-out.

After years of research, in their 1998 book *The Return of the Outlaw Billy the Kid,* Jameson and his co-author, Frederic Bean, concluded that "the case for William Henry Roberts as Billy the Kid is stronger than the case against it." They pointed out that the 1881 coroner's report never has been proved genuine, and that Pat Garrett's own word is the only real basis for believing the sheriff killed Billy the Kid. "Garrett's word was in question then and remains in question today," they wrote.

The theory offered by Roberts's supporters is that in the darkness, Pat Garrett shot an unknown, innocent cowhand, believing him to be Billy the Kid. To keep himself out of trouble, Garrett then covered up his mistake, insisting the victim was Billy.

It seems unlikely to most historians that Garrett would have been able to get away with such a cover-up. Too many people around Fort Sumner would have known the truth and exposed Garrett's scheme. It's also hard to imagine that Billy himself, with his boastful nature, would have let the public believe for long that Garrett had "gotten the drop" on him and slain him so easily. He almost certainly would have found a way to demonstrate that he remained in the land of the living and that Garrett was a liar.

Jameson also says Pat Garrett "built the Kid into a far more notorious outlaw than he actually was. By doing this, Garrett believed he [Garrett] would look good in front of the public." Almost certainly, Billy the Kid did not kill 21 men, as he claimed—a dead man for each of his birthdays. Historians believe he actually killed as few as seven men. Other western gunfighters took far more lives than Billy did; for instance, the notorious John Wesley Hardin is thought to have committed 44 murders (including that of a man whose snoring annoyed him). But Billy the Kid—perhaps largely because of Garrett's report—became more famous than all of them.

The participants in the tragic Lincoln County War for the most part went on to lead normal lives. Those who had fought on either side became ranchers, lawmen, businessmen, even government agents. The wife of lawyer McSween remarried after his death and bought a ranch; she became known as the "Cattle Queen of New Mexico." Jimmy Dolan, one of Murphy's old partners, ended up overseeing a government land office.

Pat Garrett later served as a captain in the Texas Rangers and then became a rancher. He was a celebrity and had many famous friends, including

President Theodore Roosevelt. But as the slayer of Billy the Kid, he was forever more a marked man. Many young hotheads in the Old West wanted to become famous in their own right by killing Pat Garrett.

Garrett's fate caught up with him in February 1908. While traveling by wagon from his ranch to the town of Las Cruces, New Mexico, he was shot in the back of the head. A man who worked on Garrett's ranch, Wayne Brazil, was arrested and tried for the killing. He claimed he shot Garrett in self-defense, and the jury let him go–although Garrett's pistol was still in its holster when he died. Some historians wonder whether neighboring ranchers conspired to have Garrett assassinated. In the end, his murderer was never brought to justice.

The town of Lincoln, New Mexico, in the words of one writer, "went to sleep at the close of the Lincoln County War." Murphy's once-bustling general store became a dilapidated boardinghouse; the upper floor was used occasionally as a courtroom.

As for the Kid, his legend did not die with the nighttime shoot-out in 1881 at Fort Sumner. Until the mid-1900s, as we've seen, a number of aging men claimed to be Billy the Kid. Roberts probably

was the most convincing; some historians stead-
fastly believe Roberts was indeed the Kid. Most,
though, regard all these tales as hoaxes. They con-
clude that the young fugitive named William H.
Bonney died violently, the way he had lived, at age
21 in Fort Sumner.

Chronology

1859   William H. Bonney, who would gain fame as Billy the Kid, is born in New York. (He may have been born in 1860; no one is certain of the date)

1865   Katherine McCarty Bonney moves to Indiana, taking her two sons with her; they would later move to Kansas

1873   Billy's mother marries William Antrim; the family moves to Silver City, New Mexico

1874   Billy's mother dies of tuberculosis in Silver City

1875   A prank theft results in 15-year-old Billy's first arrest— and his first escape from jail

1877   In August Billy kills Frank "Windy" Cahill, a black- smith, during an argument

1878   In February rancher John Tunstall, Billy the Kid's employer and friend, is murdered by a posse organized by his business enemies. This sets off the Lincoln County War; Billy and the Regulators kill Sheriff John Brady on April 1; Alexander McSween is killed by the Dolan-Murphy faction on July 19, ending the Lincoln County War; in the fall, Lew Wallace is appointed territorial governor of New Mexico

1879   Wallace makes a deal with Billy the Kid to obtain court testimony concerning the Lincoln County War in exchange for a pardon. Billy is arrested despite his agreement with the governor, but he escapes from jail

1880 Pat Garrett, Billy's onetime friend, is elected sheriff of Lincoln County in the fall. He sets out to capture the outlaw; in December Sheriff Garrett and a posse capture Billy and his gang at a remote place called Stinking Springs

1881 In April Billy is tried and convicted of murdering Sheriff William Brady during the Lincoln County War. He is sentenced to hang; on April 28, he slips his handcuffs, kills his guards, and escapes from jail; on July 14, Sheriff Garrett claims to have killed Billy the Kid at a Fort Sumner, New Mexico, ranch

1950 William Henry Roberts, nicknamed "Brushy Bill," claims to be Billy the Kid and asks for a pardon for his crimes

GLOSSARY

adobe–commonly used southwestern building material formed of earth and straw and baked in the sun

alias–a false name or nickname.

ambush–a surprise attack in which one person or party hides and waits for another to appear.

amnesty–official pardon for past wrongdoings.

cowpunching–a term for ranch work, or the work of a cowboy on the trail.

desperado–a bold or violent criminal; a bandit.

frontier–the area of land between unsettled and inhabited territory.

fugitive–a person wanted for a crime and hiding from law-enforcement officers.

garrison–a military post or fort.

gunslinger–a person noted for his speed and skill in handling and shooting a gun.

illegitimate–a person who is born of parents not married to each other.

illiterate–unable to read or write.

impostor–a person who deceives others by assuming a false identity.

justice of the peace–a magistrate or minor judge with limited legal authority.

monte–a card game in which players pick any two of four cards turned face up in a layout and bet that one of them will be matched before the other as cards are dealt one at a time from the pack.

pardon–forgiveness for a crime; a release from the legal penalties associated with an offense.

peers–people who are equal to others in age or status.

posse–a group of people summoned by a sheriff to help preserve the peace, usually in an emergency.

prospector–a person who explores an area looking for mineral deposits, such as gold.

rustler–a cattle thief.

siege–a blockade of a fortified place, to force those within to surrender.

stock–livestock, such as cattle and horses.

teamster–a person who drives a team of horses or other animals as an occupation.

testimony–statements made under oath to be entered into a legal record, typically in court.

testimonial–a character reference, or statement made about a person.

vigilantes–members of a group organized to punish crime, usually because ordinary legal processes seem to have failed.

FURTHER READING

Bruns, Roger A. *Billy the Kid: Outlaw of the Wild West.* Berkeley Heights, N.J.: Enslow, 2000.

Burns, Walter Noble. *The Saga of Billy the Kid.* Stamford, Conn.: Longmeadow Press, 1992 (reprint).

Garrett, Pat F. *The Authentic Life of Billy the Kid.* Norman: University of Oklahoma Press, 1988 (reprint).

Hassrick, Royal B. *Cowboys: The Real Story of Cowboys and Cattlemen.* Secaucus, N.J.: Derbibooks, 1975.

Jameson, W. C., and Frederic Bean. *The Return of the Outlaw Billy the Kid.* Plano: Republic of Texas Press, 1998.

Nolan, Frederick. *The West of Billy the Kid.* Norman: University of Oklahoma Press, 1999.

Tatum, Stephen. *Inventing Billy the Kid: Visions of the Outlaw in America.* Tucson: University of Arizona Press, 1997.

Tuska, John. *Billy the Kid.* New York: Greenwood, 1994.

Utley, Robert M. *Billy the Kid: A Short and Violent Life.* Lincoln: University of Nebraska Press, 1991.

Weddle, John, and Robert M. Utley. *Antrim Is My Stepfather's Name: The Boyhood of Billy the Kid.* Phoenix: Arizona Historical Society, 1996.

PICTURE CREDITS

DANIEL E. HARMON is associate editor of Sandlapper: The Magazine of South Carolina and editor of The Lawyer's PC, a national computer newsletter. He is the author of 21 books, most of them nonfiction historical and humorous works and biographies. Harmon lives in Spartanburg, South Carolina.